AF374795

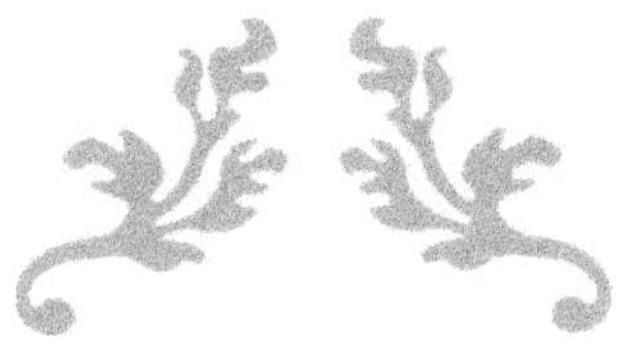

CHITTAGONG ARMOURY RAID

VOLL - 1

PRAKASH ROY

CHITTAGONG ARMOURY RAID

VOLL – I

PRAKASH ROY

Chittagong Armoury Raid

By PRAKASH ROY

First Published : May 2025

Author   : Prakash Roy

Cover   : Prakash Roy

Publication   : Notion Press

I am Prakash Roy,

I dedicate my book to all the heroes of the

Chittagong Youth Uprising -

"Those whose blood has soaked the soil of India,

"Those who, before leaving, awakened the country's youth."

Those who fought like heroes, from Chittagong to Jalalabad, from Jalalabad to Kalarpole. This book is an attempt to ensure that we do not forget the heroic stories of all those heroes. 'Vande Mataram.

Dedication

The people of India were once subjugated, the British came to this country to do business. But seeing the wealth of this country, they stayed in country. How can the wealth of this country be looted? There came a time when the country came under the British rule. There must have been many traitors behind this.

Gradually, they started ruling the entire country. How much longer would the people of India endure their slavery? We have to fight against them, we have to liberate the motherland. That is why a great struggle was waged against them. Starting from the Nil Rebellion, the Santal Rebellion, the Munda Rebellion and the Sepoy Rebellion of 1857.

Almost a hundred years have passed in this way. Then the 'Agniyuga' began. The youth of the country have awakened. From Punjab to Maharashtra, from Maharashtra to Bihar, from Bihar to Odisha, from Odisha to Assam and from Assam to the whole of Bengal. Revolutionary organizations were formed in various places. One of them was the 'Indian Republican Army.' We all know about the "Chittagong Youth Revolt" of Masterda Surya Sen. Many young people, both known and unknown, responded to his call. On April 18, 1930, the Great Revolt against the British Empire took place in Chittagong, followed by the deadly battle of Jalalabad Hills. Twelve young men lost their lives in that battle. Their biographies are presented in this book. A few days after the battle of Jalalabad Hills, the Battle of Kalarpole began, where four young revolutionaries lost their lives. The biographies of the young revolutionaries of this Kalarpole war are presented through this book. Hence the name of the book - "From Chittagong Armoury Raid." There are also life stories of several other revolutionaries. I hope the readers will enjoy reading the book and quench their thirst for knowledge.

Prakash Roy

Author Biography

Since childhood, he had a dream that he would work for the country. So he wanted to join the army. From the age of about 6-7, he wanted to know about the biographies of the country's brave warriors and freedom fighters. Our author's name is Prakash Roy. He was born on March 14, 1996 in Satvendi village of Jalpaiguri district of West Bengal. He received his first education at Panbari Barmanpara RR School, after which he joined Panbari Bhabani High School.

He tried to study a lot while fighting against family hardships, but he had to admit defeat in front of family hardships. His dream did not come true, his dream remained. Gradually, he started telling the people of the country through social media who had sacrificed for the country. We do not know about all the patriots, so he tries to present the stories of all the patriots to everyone.

Gradually, he won the hearts of many on social media and, as per the readers' wishes, he started writing books. He started writing his books and named his first Bengali book 'Khoma Nei Deshdrohi'.

I live far from the city, many have helped me in this regard. Many people have helped me with pictures of revolutionaries, and I am immensely grateful to all of them.

Jalalabad to Kalarpole
Book References:--

1. Chattogram Biplaber Banhishikha - Shachindranath Guha
2. Chattogram Yubabidroha - Ananta Singha
3. Chittagong Bidroher Kahini - Ananda Prasad Gupta
4. Chattogram Biplab - Manoranjan Ghosh
5. Muktir Sopan Jalalabad - Suresh Dey
6. Masterda Surya Sen - Swapan Mukhopadhyay
7. Nirbachita Biplobider Chelebela - Prithviraj Sen

Other books by the author:--

1. Khoma Nei Deshdrohi - Bengali
2. No Forgiveness : History of India's freedom struggle - English
3. Jalalabad Theke Kalarpole - Bengali

Table of Contents

The hero of the

Chittagong Youth Uprising

Masterda Surya Sen

Masterda Suryasen is a Bengali revolutionary who has found a place in the hearts and minds of every Bengali. He was the great hero of the Chittagong Armory attack. He was a teacher and also associated with the revolutionary party. He was called 'Masterda' because of the teacher. His organizational strength and determination were extraordinary. Let us briefly listen to the biography of Masterda Suryasen.

Surya Sen was born on March 22, 1894, in the village of Noapara in Chittagong district. His father's name was Rajmoni Sen and his mother's name was Shashibala Sen. Surya Sen is the fourth child in their family. His father died when he was only five years old. Surya Sen, who lost his parents in his childhood, was raised by his uncle Gauramani Sen. Surya Sen had a mischievous nature since childhood. However, Surya Sen was a very attentive and good student since childhood and had a serious and religious nature.

He would not remain silent in the face of anyone's troubles. He always stood by the side of people. That's why the elders used to say about him, this boy will grow up to make the country and its name shine. But this prediction came true.

He once taught at a high school in Chittagong. At that time, he formed a revolutionary group with school and college students. In 1919, unarmed people were shot at in Jallianwala Bagh. In protest, Rabindranath Tagore renounced his "knighthood". A wave of revolution spread throughout the country. At that time, the masterda had only one thing to say: the British needed only weapons to teach them the right lessons. Many young people joined this revolutionary group, including revolutionaries like Ambika Chakraborty, Ananta Singh, Ganesh Ghosh, Loknath Bal, Nirmal Sen, Tarakeswar Dastidar, and Pritilata Waddedar.

Money is needed for the armed struggle, it will come from words. Government revenue will have to be looted as per the Masterdar's orders. December 23, 1923. The revolutionaries looted the money from the railway company's cars and fled towards the jungle.

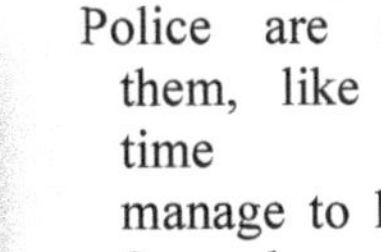

Police are after them, like this time they manage to hide. Several days passed. Then he started planning again. He formed a revolutionary group. He decided that this time they would attack the government arsenal and other communication facilities together. The date was fixed on April 18, 1930. This was the historic attack, the Chittagong Armory attack. That day came, and more than 50-60 young men came out. Attacks began, railways, telephone exchanges were destroyed. The British arsenal was looted.

There, a pitched battle with the British police began, in which they were quite successful. Under the leadership of Surya Sen, the city of Chittagong was free and independent from the British for several days. But the revolutionaries were forced to retreat. In the darkness of night, they went out into the forest of the mountains. Finally, the revolutionaries took refuge in the Jalalabad hills. The day was April 22nd, just four days after the attack on Chittagong, the battle between the British army and the rebels began. Twelve revolutionaries died in that war. In the end they have to walk behind even now. Even then, they waged a guerrilla war for three long years.

The police were searching for Masterda. They announced that they would give a reward of ten thousand taka if they could catch him. Masterda had miraculously escaped arrest several times.

But there was no final escape. At that time, Masterda was hiding in a house in the village. Masterda Suryasen was arrested for treachery, The day was February 16, 1933. This time the trial verdict sentenced Masterdar's colleague Tarkeshwar Dastidar to death and Kalpana Dutta to life imprisonment. And the verdict of our Masterda Suryasen's trial was death sentence.

That day came, January 12, 1934. Before Masterda Suryasen was brought to the gallows, unspeakable torture was inflicted on him. The infamous butchers of the British smashed his teeth with a hammer. There, Masterda was almost dead. He was hanged unconscious. Tarakeswar Dastidar was hanged along with him. Following his example, many young men have sung the song of victory for life on the gallows.

Chittagong Armory Attack

Hero Youth Himanshu Sen (Ashu)

Himanshu Sen was the same age as Ananda Gupta. They studied together in the minor school in their childhood. Since then, Himanshu did not give up easily in sports, whether it was fighting. His skills in horse riding, gun shooting were extraordinary.

April 18, 1930, two hours left. A car has not yet been arranged.

At any rate, a motor car must be arranged at this time. Ananta ran to the road to Ganesh's house. On his way, he met Ambika Chakraborty in front of the telegraph office. Ananta opened up about the problem. Ambika took the problem seriously and said, "There's nothing to worry about - everything will be fine. I believe you can find a car. There's no time, hurry up - we're waiting here safely."

Ananda and Ananta ran at high speed again. They picked up Himanshu on the road. Himanshu hears all the happenings and also learns that the attack time has been postponed for him by two hours. Hearing all these incidents, Himanshu got upset and said, "How beautifully you have been organizing the work for so long! At the last minute, the car problem and the attack were also postponed. I don't feel good about either of them. I feel very uncomfortable."

Young Himanshu was not short of courage and bravery. Out of the five who attacked the police line, Himanshu was the first to be selected. Standing alongside Ananta and Ganesh, Himanshu attacked bravely. Not everyone has the courage to stand in front of a gun. That Himanshu can even give his life while laughing.

To ease Himanshu's discomfort, Ananta Singh said, "Ashu, (Himanshu's nickname) look, our path is inaccessible and dangerous. We have to follow a winding path." It is foolish to always think of Smooth Sailing. The main lesson of strategy is - no matter how difficult the problem is, it must be solved. Don't get upset. "It is not fitting for those who possess such overall power in the organization to give up on this minor problem." Ananta tried to convince Himanshu by saying many more things.

Himanshu understood after hearing Ananta's words. Himanshu understood his mistake and stopped Ananta and said - "I made a mistake. I have temporarily lost this key quality of a revolutionary soldier." Courage to embrace death is not everything - determination to solve problems is also essential. Tell me what to do." Ananta happily said - "I want this!" Ananda Gupta also joined Ananta and said - "This is our Ashu!"

As they spoke, they reached Ganesh's house. "Not a single taxi to be found. All Nikhin-Banga are engaged in Muslim Conference. Ananda Gupta will return to Ambika Chakraborty with the car at that time. Ananta asked Himanshu to go with Ananda Gupta. Ananda will drop Himanshu at the taxi stand near Laldighi. Ananta said to Himanshu very seriously - "You must get a taxi by any means - at any price." You have to come here (at Ganesh Ghosh's house) by taxi within an hour, or else by 9:30. Remember, Impossible is the word found in the dictionary of fools!"

Himanshu understood Ananta's words to the core. Before Ananta Singh finished speaking, Ananda said - "He will definitely bring Ekta Taxi." "Kire Ashu, Can you? - surely can." While leaving, Himanshu firmly told everyone - by all means he will bring a taxi from wherever he is within the stipulated time. Then he set off towards Laldighi.

The attack on Chittagong armory began. Twice in a row there was a skirmish between the British forces and the revolutionaries, the British forces were defeated both times. None of the revolutionaries suffered a single scratch. There is no point in wasting time, the more time the enemy gets, the more opportunities he will get.

Masterda gave the order - "Pour petrol - set it on fire!" Himanshu started spreading petrol with one more person, petrol was spread well in all armoury, guardroom and magazine room. Himanshu would set fire this time, standing in the petrol-soaked Armory premises, he lit a match and went to set fire. Himanshu's clothes were also quite wet with petrol, the over-enthusiastic young man didn't notice that. As soon as the fire was lit, the armory, guard room, and magazine room burst into flames with a loud bang. Just like that, Himanshu's body caught fire in the blink of an eye. Himanshu is no longer seen in the crowd of fire. His cries are heard, he is running here and there. Naresh Roy and Bibhu Bhattacharya, both of whom were qualified doctors, rushed to Himanshu. But there was no way to put out the fire. Seeing no other option, Naresh and Bibhu asked Himanshu to lie down on the ground and roll over. Himanshu did so and Naresh and Bibhu went ahead to put out the fire.

Himanshu was on fire for about a minute. The extent of the injuries was beyond the imagination of any of the revolutionaries. Ananta Singh, Ganesh Ghosh and Makhan Ghoshal together put Himanshu in the car and started for home. He dropped Himanshu off near Ananda's house. Ananda's house is near Himanshu's house. No sound of his moans could be heard in the car. Perhaps Himanshu's regret for his mistake knew no bounds. So he might have endured the burn with his mouth shut.

Himanshu went down in silence. None of Ganesh, Ananta, or Makhan consoled him or even said goodbye. In their busyness, they forgot to say goodbye.

On April 19, Himanshu, who was near death, was captured by the police. Immediately after being captured, he was sent to the Chittagong Jail Hospital for treatment. But by then, Himanshu's condition had become beyond treatment. Finally, on April 20, Himanshu Sen died in the hospital.

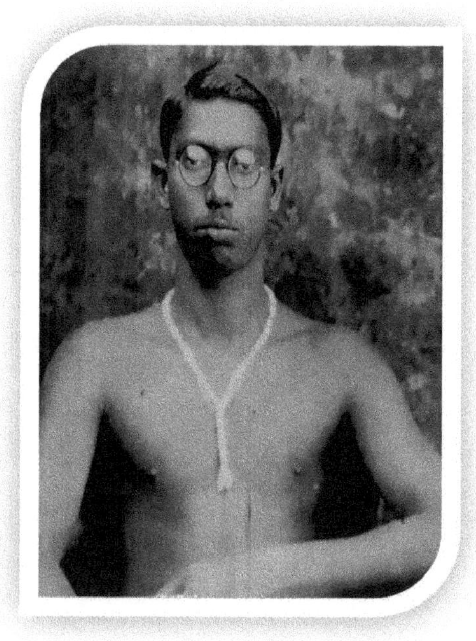

Ananta Singh

Harigopal Bal & Moti Kanungo

Naresh Roy, Tripura Sen & Bidhu Bhattacharya

Jiten Das, Madhu Dutta & Pulin Ghosh

Prabhas Bal, Shashanka Dutta & Nirmal Lala

Harigopal Bal (Tegra)

That historic day was 18th April 1930, when the Chittagong Arsenal was attacked on the orders of Masterda Surya Sen. This 18th April will always be remembered in the hearts of Bengalis, for they were able to keep Chittagong free from the British for several days. Exactly four days later, the terrible battle of Jalalabad began, in which several young men lost their lives. I am going to talk about one such young man. His name is Harigopal Bal (Tegra), the younger brother of the revolutionary leader of Chittagong, Loknath Bal. Harigopal Bal was born in Pathar Ghata, Dhorala, Chittagong. His father's name was Prankrishna Bal. He studied in a municipal school, and Tegra, the younger son of Prankrishna Bal, a responsible government employee, had to grow up under strict discipline.

In the meantime, he kept in touch with Masterda Surya Sen's revolutionary group. Tegra was as beautiful to look at as he was intelligent. He gradually made his way into the minds of the revolutionary leaders. The revolutionary leader Masterda Surya Sen's goal was to attack the Chittagong arsenal. Weapons were needed to fight the British. A group of young men were assigned to attack the European Club. Great British gentlemen lived there. The British sahebs were rejoicing there after dusk.

Masterda's dream was to destroy this European Club. Chosen Tegra along with some other revolutionary youth. On 18th April 1930, everyone left for the European Club. But since it was Good Friday, the European Club was closed that day. So that day they returned with a broken heart. After the attack on the Chittagong arsenal, they set out in the dark of night for safe shelter. A few miles away from the city was the Jalalabad hill, where they took shelter.

No food, no sleep, the chest is bursting with thirst. There is water a little further down the mountain, but going there is a disaster. If you go there, you might get noticed by someone. Tegra once said to his grandfather Loknath Bal - "I am very hungry, Sonada." Loknath Bal was one of the party presidents. He said - "Brother, how can the revolutionaries be so bitter?"

The day was 22nd April, the historic battle started between the British forces and the rebels. Although the smoke of gunpowder was dark all around, there was no sign of a ceasefire. Why is the enemy's machine gun still not stopping? The machine gun's muzzle flashes are visible from the top of the hill. The Tegra have forgotten about their own self-defense, they have forgotten military principles. Not afraid of death, Tegra is shooting by aiming at the flash of fire in the muzzle of the machine gun. Since he

cannot aim while lying down, he occasionally jumps up and shoots. When Nirmal sees him, he shouts - "What are you doing? Why are you standing and firing?" Tegra replies - "The British have to silence the machine guns."

Nirmal gave the fearless Tegra complete freedom to fight, relying on his own intelligence, will, and courage. He only gave a little warning. The machine gun bullets were coming in droves, and Tegra was reckless at that time. Just as strategy and tactics are necessary for victory in war, courage, bravery, and soldierly morale are no less essential.

Tegra's hand gun roared like a roaring lion, leaping and firing. Tegra was not saved in the last time. A barrage of machine gun bullets came and wounded Tegra and left. Machine gun fire greeted Tegra as if wearing the wreath of valor.

Tegra fell to the ground, his body covered in blood. He was still holding the gun tightly, his eyes wide open. He wanted to say something but couldn't. With great difficulty, Dada Lokenath said to Bal - "Sonada, I am leaving, Masterda, farewell! Brother, to all the enemies...." He could not say anything else. Perhaps he wanted to say - "There is no forgiveness for the enemies, there is no mercy for them." The entire Jalalabad hills echoed - "No mercy, no compassion - no forgiveness for the enemy."

"Sonada, I am going" - "Tegra's call had reached the ears of Dada Loknath Ball. At that time Loknath replied - "There is no one called Sonada in the field of war. We are Sonic, our duty is 'do or die'! Give life like a hero."

He did not move from his place, nor did he become agitated. Friends from all sides shouted - "Tegra has left us, Tegra is no longer with us." Together, everyone's voices filled the sky and air - "Long Live Tegra! Long Live Revolution! Long Live Revolutionary Tegra! Vande Mataram."

Tegra was the first to die in the battle of Jalalabad hills. He woke everyone up by saying - "There is no forgiveness for the enemy." He was estimated to have been only 14 years old at the time of his death.

Tripura Sen

Many of us today do not try to remember those heroes whose blood turned the Jalalabad hills red. Yes, I am talking about the Jalalabad battle from Chittagong. The hero was Masterda Surya Sen, under his leadership Chittagong Armory was attacked. One of those who died participating in the battle of Jalalabad was Tripura Sen.

Tripura Sen was born on May 22, 1913, in the village of Sonaranga in Bikrampur Pargana, Dhaka district. His father's name was Nibaran Chandra Sen. He studied at the municipal school. At one time, the student wore the uniform of a brigadier of the Volunteer Force, looking like a British officer, making it difficult for everyone to recognize him. He was one of the enthusiastic young members of the Sadarghat Club. Just as he was tall, 5 feet 8 inches, so was his fair complexion, very handsome. As calm as Tripura was, he was also extraordinary in intellect.

Tripura has had a lot of organizing skills since he was a ninth grader. She had an influence on all the students of the municipal school. A sensational scene took place on the death anniversary of the great revolutionary of the freedom struggle, Jatin Das. That day, the school was almost closed, a strike began. But all the students of the municipal school were silent, but Tripura came out of the class and told everyone - "Students, come out today, otherwise revolutionary Jatin Das will be disrespected. I will not let that happen."

On that day, the strike called for as the day of death, no student could stay in the class. Everyone had to come out. No one could stop him that day, from that day on he got the place of a good leader of the Chittagong student society. Even though he was a 15-year-old teenager at that time. He had many such identities before, Tripura attracted everyone's attention as a lieutenant of the Volunteers' Force during the Chittagong Youth Conference. From then on, everyone called him Lieutenant Tripura.

In May 1929, the Congress Conference was held in Chittagong. The God of Revolution, Netaji Subhas Chandra Bose, came to preside over the Chittagong District Congress Conference. Masterda Surya Sen, Ananta Singh, Ganesh Ghosh and Kishore Tripura Sen were present at this conference. They informed Subhas Bose that they did not support the Congress's policy of non-violence and that they were preparing for armed rebellion.

It was decided that the Chittagong Arsenal would be attacked on 18th April 1930. A few days before the Chittagong Arsenal attack, Tripura took the matriculation examination. Kishore Tripura Sen participated as a young member of the revolutionary party. But they could not succeed in the attack, he could not accept this failure from his heart. Tripura Sengupta carried out the task assigned to attack the armory with due diligence. He was given the responsibility of collecting news from the telegraph and telephone offices.

After the attack on the Chittagong arsenal, they set out in search of safe shelter. They entered the mountains and jungles. After crossing high and low hills all day, they all took shelter in the Jalalabad hills, a few miles from the city.

The revolutionaries understood that war was inevitable, but how long would it last due to hunger and sleeplessness. As time goes by, they will become weaker. Otherwise, they would enter the city before him and start a rebellion. Tripura was the Group Brigadier, he went to Masterda Surya Sen and said - "Masterda, we should not wait any longer. The longer we delay, the more the enemy will gain the advantage in battle. We have to enter the city and attack tonight. You give final orders in this regard."

Masterda said with a smile - "Yes brother, yes, today we will try to attack the enemy stronghold of the city. I also agree with you. Offence is the best of Defence. Defensive war would be a fatal mistake for us. Rest assured, we will take a decision now."

The day was 22nd April, the battle of Jalalabad hill front was organized. Tripura was burning like fire, he fought with a rifle in one hand. It seems like a truly seasoned soldier. He was only 17 years old, and he served as a commander in the victorious army. Tripura is by no means silent, the war continues. But who knows when death will come, a swarm of bullets from the British army came and left, piercing the chest. Tripura was still standing. He fell to the ground as soon as he moved. As soon as the bullet hit him, his entire face turned white, as if there was not a drop of blood in his body. But the strange thing was - the gun was still in his hand, tightly grasped.

Clinging to the hills of Jalalabad, Tripura bid farewell forever, everyone shouted - 'Long Live Tripura! Long Live Revolution! Long Live Revolutionary Tripura! Vande Mataram.'

Even in the face of death, Tripura said to his fellow warriors - "Continue the fight, victory is not far away." He slowly closed his eyelids and embraced death.

Nirmal Lala

Nirmal Lala was the youngest fighter in the Battle of Jalalabad Hills. He was born in a middle-class family in Boalkhali Upazila of Chittagong. Fatherless, Nirmal grew up under the care and affection of his elder sister. His primary education was at Cox's Bazar High School. Nirmal was just a student of the eighth grade, at that time he was only fourteen years old. Sitting by the sea in Cox's Bazar, he dreams of freeing the subjugated country from the oppression of the British and establishing an independent country.

Two months left for the Chittagong Armory attack. At that time, Nirmal Lala came in contact with Bidhu Sen and other revolutionaries in Cox's Bazar. He was desperate to see the party's main leader, Masterda Surya Sen. One day, he himself took the initiative and rushed to Chittagong city to meet Masterda.

Masterda started planning to attack the Chittagong arsenal. Nirmal realized after a few days there that something was going to happen soon. He ran straight to Masterda and pleaded, "You guys will do something soon, I understand." "But you have to take me with you." Masterda felt amused after hearing Nirmal's words. Eighth grade student, only fourteen years old he claims: Masterda laughingly asked - "How long have you been to the party?"Nirmal said - "It's been about two months."

Masterda said again - "Which class are you in?"

Nirmal said - "Class eight."

Masterda said - "How old are you?"

Nirmal said - "Fourteen."

Masterda said again - "How can you go with us at such a young age?" Despite many attempts, he could not convince Masterda, so Nirmal returned to Cox's Bazar in a state of dismay. After leaving, he told Bidhu Sen - "Bidhu, no matter what, I will go with you. Is there no way to convince Masterda?"

Bidhu Sen saw that his condition was like a madman, and understanding his gravity, he said - "You go and catch Masterda again. Besides, I can't find any other way." Nirmal rushed back to Chittagong. Before leaving, he made a promise that he would never return to Cox's Bazar. The day before leaving Cox's Bazar, he called his classmates and friends and distributed all his books and notebooks. When everyone asked the reason for this donation, he said - "I am leaving Cox's Bazar. I don't think I will return."

He had a very dear little suitcase, which he also gave to his friend. He rushed to the Congress office in Chittagong city near Masterda. He told all the events and also told about leaving Cox's Bazar. He also said - this time he is determined, he will not accept any word. Masterda stayed behind, finally Masterda was forced to accept Nirmal's offer.

The day was April 18, 1930, and he was in the police line attack. After capturing the Chittagong armory, they left the police line before dawn on April 19 and entered the mountains and jungles. After crossing high and low hills all day, they all settled down in a secluded place a few miles from the city. Everyone was tired of going from one end of the mountain to the other. Then Masterda called Nirmal and said affectionately - "Nirmal, you will not be able to bear this hunger, lack of water, sleeplessness and running around day and night at this age. You are a village boy, the police do not know you. You should go home."

Nirmal said - "Masterda, I have not come to return home. What will I do with this life after returning home? I will spend the last drop of blood in my body for the work of the country. This is the goal of my life. Haven't I read in the Gita. "Sharirani bihaay jirna nananyani nabani sanyaati dehi."

The day was April 22nd, a fierce battle had begun between the British army and the revolutionaries. There was a continuous rain of bullets on both sides. No one has any fear, no care. Suddenly a bullet came and went through the chest of Nirmal Lala. As soon as the bullet hit her, she jumped up - she could only stand for a short time. Everyone's eyes fell on him - lie down, lie down, don't stand up or you'll get shot. In a short time, he was rolling. Blood was pouring from Nirmal's wound. Saroj Guha and Group Commander Deboprasad Gupta were next to him. Nirmal couldn't say anything. He seemed to be trying to stand up, leaning on his gun, but he couldn't. Group Commander Deboprasad Gupta, who was nearby, did not care about death, but ran to Nirmal amidst the heavy firing. Deboprasad carefully picked up Nirmal's head, began to caress his head with utmost affection. It was a wonderful sight. Nirmal was unconscious, but perhaps feeling the affectionate touch, she thought of her mother. Nirmal laid her head on Deboprasad Gupta's lap and said goodbye forever.

For the last time, his young voice uttered 'Vande Mataram.' Then his blood-soaked body lay clinging to the ground of Jalalabad.

Pulinchandra Ghosh

The name "Jalalabad" is known to all, this Jalalabad Hill Chittagong Youth Rebellion was reddened by the blood of some revolutionaries. Everyone knows the name of Masterda Surya Sen, he was one of the great heroes of this party. It was under his orders that one campaign after another was launched, from the attack on Chittagong Armory to Jalalabad and from there to Kalarpole and then various other campaigns.

Pulinchandra Ghosh was one of the revolutionaries who died in the battle of Jalalabad Hills. Revolutionary Pulinchandra Ghosh was born in Gonsaidanga, Chittagong. His father's name was Jagatchandra Ghosh. Pulinchandra Ghosh's education was very good, for which he had a good reputation, but the poverty and hardship of the family were not very good.

He had to study by fighting against the poverty and hardships of the family. In his early life, he was a student of J. M. Sen School. He was very intelligent and a young revolutionary. Even the British government's spies could not catch him, he disappeared in the blink of an eye by putting dust in their eyes.

A very interesting incident happened one day. Pulinchandra Ghosh was riding a bicycle very fast. When the detectives followed him with a spy, to see where he was going and what he was doing. The detective's spy was behind him, Pulinchandra Ghosh suddenly disappeared. British government intelligence is shocked. This is how he won the heart of Masterda Suryasen, the hero of Chittagong Armory attack.

He was involved in social service from a young age. He was also a volunteer at the Ramakrishna Ashram. Sometimes he would be seen carrying a begging bag, begging and donating to the ashram.

While begging, a gentleman called out to Pullin and asked, "Well, you always talk about freedom, what would you do if you got this freedom?" Pullin replied, "If I get freedom, I won't have to beg forAlms for others."

They would fight against the British, but they did not have such firearms. Masterda Suryasen began to plan a new campaign, finally deciding to attack the Chittagong arsenal. At that time, he, i.e. Pulinchandra, was a student of class 10.

The day was 18th April 1930, in this historic operation, Pulinchandra Ghosh participated in the capture of the Police Lines armoury on behalf of the Indian Republican Army. Then they went out in the darkness of the night towards the Jalalabad hills.

On April 21st, Pulin was so weak from hunger and thirst that he didn't even have the strength left to walk a short distance to get some water from a spring. Unable to bear the burning thirst any longer, what did Pulin do? He opened a can of lubricating oil and poured it into his mouth. As soon as the oil entered his stomach, he couldn't bear it anymore and immediately started vomiting. She was sick and even sicker. Her uncle's house was nearby in the village of Fatehabad. Seeing her physical condition, she was asked to go to her uncle's house. But she did not agree. She said, "I cannot go anywhere leaving everyone like this."

On April 22nd, armed British forces arrived at the Jalalabad hills, and fighting began on both sides. After participating in the first and second battles, they emerged victorious as a powerful revolutionary group. Then the third battle began, and bullets were raining down on the Jalalabad hills. Pulinchandra Ghosh was gradually advancing towards the British forces with his gun, and the continuous firing continued.

The entire Jalalabad hills were covered in gun smoke. There was no sign of stopping the war. Pulin was next to Loknath Bal. Loknath's chest was bursting with thirst for water. There was no water anywhere. Pulin understood that Loknathdar was thirsty. So he said - "Lokada, I have a fresh mango. Take the mango - eat it, it will quench your thirst."

Lokenath said, "You keep it for now, we'll see later. We'll share it or we'll both eat it." The machine gun fire continued. It was dangerous to move around, you never knew when the bullet would hit. When the machine gun's cartridge belt ran out, it took a while to change another one. The mango could be put to good use at that opportunity. Lokenath looked at Pulin for the mango, just at that moment a volley of bullets came and shattered Pulin's entire body. Pulin immediately fell to the ground - the gun was lying beside him. Pulin was lying there, covered in blood, with the mango in his hand, and his hand extended towards Lokenath. Lokenath had said that the two of them would share the food - who would he share it with now? Tears welled up in Lokenath's eyes.

How much compassion did Pulin have for Loknath, he would give the raw mango he had kept for himself to 'Lokada' - he would be happy if he ate 'Lokada'. The mango in Pulin's hand was soaked in blood, he had kept it carefully, thinking that he would eat 'Lokada'. If Loknath did not eat the mango, Pulin's last wish would be insulted. So Loknath took the blood-stained mango from his hand and ate it. This was the story of the revolutionary Pulin Ghosh.

Shashanka Shekhar Dutta

We all know more or less the historic operation that took place on 18th April 1930. That day, the Chittagong armoury was attacked. Among the revolutionaries who took part was Shashanka Shekhar Dutta. Everyone calls him Shashanka for short. Shashanka Dutta was born in 1912 in the village of Dengapara in Chittagong (British India, present-day Bangladesh). His father's name was Manindralal Dutta. Shashanka Dutta was a second-year student of Dhaka College. He was an intermediate student of Chittagong College.

On one hand, the unspeakable oppression of the British was increasing, and on the other hand, the armed struggle of the freedom fighters. Suddenly, when he became interested in revolution, he joined the revolutionary party.

Joining the revolutionary party of Masterda Surya Sen, he became a member of the "Indian Republican Army." He was eager to help the revolutionary party in every way. As I have already said, we all know about the Chittagong Youth Rebellion, the Chittagong armory was attacked as per the orders of Masterda Surya Sen. In the end, the revolutionaries were able to escape from there and took refuge in the Jalalabad hills.

In the darkness of the night, the revolutionaries ran wherever their eyes could see. Exactly four days after the attack on the Chittagong Arsenal, that is, on April 22, 1930, it is known that three consecutive battles took place on the top of the Jalalabad hill. Twice they defeated the British army. For the third time, another battle began, their final battle, a very terrible battle. Shashanka Dutt had endless laughter, enthusiasm and indomitable courage in his eyes.

He will never be defeated by the enemy. It is truly unbelievable that an 18-year-old young man could utter "Vande Mataram" in a moment and hold a rifle in his hand. The war seems to have no end, the endless rain of bullets continues. But no one knows when death hangs over someone's head in the war. But in the endless war of that day, a total of 12 young men died. During the war, a machine gun bullet came out and swallowed Shashanka Shekhar Dutt. He immediately collapsed in the lap of death.

The body was so dismembered by the machine gun fire that no one could recognize Shashanka Dutt and Madhu Dutta after seeing the picture. Who are they?

That day, the lap of Jalalabad hills turned red with the blood of the revolutionaries. We were blessed, our motherland was blessed with their blood. Without their sacrifice, we would not have achieved freedom. I bow down to the feet of all the heroes of the Jalalabad battle.

Madhusudan Dutta

The incident of attack on Chittagong Armory is probably known to all of us. For which he was able to keep Chittagong independent during the British rule for a few days. Yes, I am talking about that Chittagong, one of whose main leaders we know the name of Masterda Surya Sen. At his call, more than 60 teenagers and young men were inspired by the mantra of revolution.

Among them who participated in the battle of Jalalabad and achieved valor, I am going to talk about one of the martyrs there.

The name of the person I am talking about is Madhusudan Dutta. He was born in a place called Bidgram in Chittagong. His father's name was Manindra Kumar Dutta. The boy had revolutionary thoughts since childhood. Inspired by Ramakrishna Biswas, a school student of Sarwatoli village, the teenaged young man Madhusudan Dutta joined the revolutionary group.

They lacked nothing in the world, yet his mind wanted to breathe freedom. We must stand against the British in this country, only then will everyone be able to breathe freely one day. He was known as a very old worker of the revolutionary party. Madhusudan Dutta started his political career from 1921 to 1922.

In the year 1924, the revolutionary leaders and some members were all imprisoned one by one. He took all the work of the revolution on his own shoulders. He went to different places and schools and colleges and started promoting the revolution. The people of the house came to know this news, so then he was sent to Jamshedpur. It is heard that he used to work there, he went there and worked as a coal contractor. And he used to bring all the money to the revolutionary group.

He returned to Chittagong on April 1, 1930. Then, according to Masterda Surya Sen's plan, he decided to attack the Chittagong armory. At that time, his revolutionary friends thought that they would no longer have him as a fellow fighter in the attack on the arsenal. Now their doubts were dispelled, and after returning to Chittagong on April 1, he again jumped into the revolutionary work.

Before the attack on Chittagong Armory, they faced financial problems, so they all helped by giving whatever money they could. The revolutionary Madhusudan Dutta brought home ornaments and money to their group. The day was 18th April 1930, what did he do before the attack on the Chittagong Armory, he also brought his home gun to the revolutionaries. In this operation, he joined the attack on the police line.

Madhu was the son of a rich landlord, he lacked nothing. He was far above the common people. Wealth could not touch him, what touched him was the independence of the country. That is why he jumped into the Chittagong Great Rebellion. That day, they broke down the door of the armory and took possession of the police line along with rifles, revolvers and cartridges. As the master had said, they found the British Union Jack and set it on fire. There, the revolutionaries had to engage in light fighting.

This time, the national flag was raised in celebration of victory. A salute was given by firing three guns into the open sky. Then they left there in the darkness of night. Despite the darkness all around, their eyes crossed the mountains and forests and finally took refuge in the Jalalabad hills. Four days passed there.

The day was April 22, 1930, they were present on the top of the Jalalabad hill. They were all exhausted by hunger and thirst for water that day. Meanwhile, a group of British soldiers arrived. In the meantime, the historic battle of the Jalalabad hill began. They were impatient due to hunger and thirst for water, but still they were fighting like a true seasoned soldier.

They only had guns in their hands, and the British army had brought cartridges and machine guns that fired many bullets at once. The revolutionaries were victorious in the first and second battles, and darkness descended on them in the third battle. Suddenly a bunch of machine gun fire came and gave the revolutionary Madhusudan Dutt the garland of heroism. He immediately fell down in the lap of Jalalabad hill. Madhusudan Dutta bid farewell to his revolutionary friends.

Prabhas Chandra Bal

The Chittagong Arsenal attack was a historic campaign against the British. And as one of the main leaders of this group, we know about Masterda Surya Sen. Under his leadership, one after another campaign was carried out on the British camps. His special operations included the attack on the Chittagong Arsenal and the Battle of Jalalabad. A number of young men lost their lives participating in this Jalalabad battle.

The person I am going to talk about here today is Prabhas Bal. He was born in Dhorala, Chittagong and his father's name was Manomohan Bal. He was a student of Chittagong J. M. Sen School. He is the cousin of Loknath Bal, the leader of the Chittagong Arsenal attack, and Harigopal Bal, the martyr of Jalalabad.

It is said that his ancestor used to apply oil on his body while bathing, and when he asked for oil from the householder, the householder would hand over a whole mustard seed. He would rub it and extract oil from it. From then on, the householder gave him the title "Bal". He came to be known as Bal from Basu.

Exercises were taught at the Vrindavan Ashram, and the editor of that exercise was Prabhas Bal. His teacher was Ananta Singh, who used to go there every Sunday and give training. Ananta Singh, seeing the strength of Prabhas Bal's body, thought that if the strength of this great hero is not used for the motherland, then of what use will this hero's strength be. He gradually made Prabhas a fan of revolution, and then introduced him to Masterda Surya Sen.

In 1929, in the Chittagong District Congress elections, Prabhas Bal campaigned for the revolutionary party along with Ananta Singh. No food, no bathing, just work and work. He made members of those who were not Congress members before. Prabhas' campaign opens the door to Masterda's victory.

He had a good reputation in the sports community, Prabhas was a very good football player. Apart from Anant Singh, his path of revolutionary life was followed by Kali Chakraborty (Kali Chakraborty was a revolutionary who participated in the Chittagong Armory attack). One day, Kali saw Prabhas smoking a cigarette with him, at that time, according to the revolutionaries, smoking cigarettes was forbidden. Then Kali called him and said - "You have to stop smoking, tell me today whether you will keep my word." Prabhas did not say yes or no. Prabhas said - "Give me time to think! If I tell you now out of shame that I will quit smoking, if I cannot quit later, then promising you to stop smoking will be the biggest sin."

Two days later, Prabhas promised Kali - "I promise you that I will never smoke cigarettes with anyone else." Indeed, he never touched a cigarette again. He kept this promise until his death. Congress leader Mahim Das brought the Congress establishment from the clutches of Tripura Chowdhury to young leaders interested in the freedom struggle. That day, he won the heart of Masterda Surya Sen.

After this, Masterdar ordered that the Chittagong arsenal should be attacked, if the fight against the British was to be fought in the interest of defending the motherland. The date was fixed for 18th April 1930. On that day, he participated in the attack on the Auxiliary Force arsenal.

Finally, they set off towards the Jalalabad hills in the darkness of night. Four days later, on April 22, a face-to-face battle with the British forces began. On one side, a large British force with machine guns and on the other, the revolutionaries with rifles. Prabhas fought bravely in the first and second battles. He fought bravely in the third battle and, fighting like a hero, he was shot dead on the Jalalabad hills and died on the spot.

Thus, how many unknown young men embraced death for the freedom of the country.

Loknath Bal

Naresh Roy

The history of the freedom struggle is still unknown to us. Especially, we still do not know about all the revolutionaries who attacked the Chittagong Arsenal. Among all those revolutionaries who participated in the battle of Jalalabad and died, one of them is Naresh Roy. They fought like heroes and embraced death, in the interest of protecting the motherland.

Revolutionary Naresh Roy was born in Noapara, Kendua Upazila, Netrokona district. His father's name was Girish Chandra Roy. He was the youngest son of Girish Chandra Roy. He was very good at his studies, he had many names as a talented student. He studied in the village school. After that, he was admitted to Edward School in Mymensingh town. During his studies, he was honored as the best fist fighter.

Mymensingh passed his matriculation with honors from Edward School in the city. Then he went to Chittagong to study medicine and was admitted to Chittagong National Medical School. It was in Chittagong that he found a new path in life. Gradually, he came in contact with Ananta Singh and joined the revolutionary group of Masterda Surya Sen.

He was unique in courage and efficiency, and as a result of his extraordinary activities he held the favorite place of Ananta Singh and Ganesh Ghosh. He was a very calm person, never getting angry even in the face of hundreds of problems. That is why he is loved by everyone.

Naresh Roy's contribution to every important work of the party was special. He was in charge of creating clubs in their neighborhoods. According to the plan of the Chittagong Youth Rebellion, he was given a special task, he was given the responsibility of leading the attack on the European Club. He was a trustworthy worker of all the members of the party, so everyone trusted him. So Masterda appointed him to keep an eye on the spies. Naresh's activities were such that the police had to play the fool again and again.

In 1930, revolutionary Tarkeshwar Dastidar was seriously injured while preparing explosives at the Chittagong Congress office. To hide him from the city to the village, Naresh Roy of Medical College, Bidhu Bhattacharya, Jatin Das of Mahira village and Sushil De of Dhorla village came to Kheyaghat with Tarkeshwar. To raise Tarakeswar to the sampan. A group of local people blocked the road before arriving at Kheyaghat. They became suspicious when they saw Tarakeswar in a bandage.

Seeing that Bidhu Bhattacharya, Naresh Roy and the revolutionaries were late in returning, Ananta Singh and Ganesh Ghosh came to see him. Seeing the crowd, Ananta and Ganesh shouted loudly - "Kon hai?" Immediately people blocking the road ran away in fear. Then Tarakeswar was lifted into a sampan.

After this, it was confirmed that the Chittagong armory would have to be attacked. This time, we would have to fight them with their own weapons.

Various plans are being made for the attack. It's ok to attack, but it takes two cars. They want to keep the car under their control for three hours by rendering the driver unconscious with chloroform. They have given the responsibility of testing this chloroform to 'Gold Medalist' students of the medical college, Naresh Roy and Bidhu Bhattacharya.

The day was April 18, 1930, the day before the attack, Ananta Singh dropped Ambika Chakraborty off in front of the Congress office, then saw Naresh Roy on the road to Ganesh's house.

Ananta Singh said to Naresh - "Is everything okay, Naresh? Have you personally checked all the weapons there? Is everything okay?"

Naresh replied - "Yes, everything is fine."

Ananta Singh repeated - "You say there is no doubt? Not a single one will fail during the attack - are you sure?"

Naresh said - "Yes, I am sure."

Ananta said - "How is the morale of everyone in your team?"

Naresh said - "Very good, excellent! There is a competition among them - 'Who will sacrifice their life first---."

Naresh Roy was leading the attack on the European Club. Ananta had nothing to say to Naresh, but to gain some strength, he said to Naresh - "Remember, Naresh, our sacrifice will never be in vain! Today we are going to take revenge for the oppression we have suffered so far - I need strength, I need courage, - and I need indomitable morale." "Look, Naresh, don't let anyone break down at the last moment. Go and tell them - no mercy, no compassion, not a single bit of pity! I want revenge - I just want ruthless revenge! - Revenge for the hanging of Khudiram, Kanailal - Revenge for the murder of children and women in Jallianwala Bagh."

Naresh's two eyes were burning like fire. It was time to teach the British a lesson. They have done so much injustice to the people of India. Now, this is the opportunity to take revenge. Naresh firmly told Ananta Singh - "Today, the British rulers will understand that not only they have the exclusive right to oppress, we also have it." Today they too will see how cruel we can be - how ruthless and how tough we are. Today they will have to atone for their sins by shedding their blood. God will not forgive those who have neglected the commandments of Jesus, the Savior of mankind! The horror of death that we will create today will warn the British rulers for the future - The consequences of their unjust oppression will be even more sinister and more inauspicious."

At night, the revolutionaries set out on a new campaign. Naresh Roy was given the responsibility of leading the attack on the European Club. Under his leadership, Tripura Sen, Deboprasad Gupta, Amarendra Nandi, Biren Dey and Manoranjan Sen went to the European Club with bombs and weapons to avenge the Jallianwala Bagh massacre. But they returned slowly. There was no enthusiasm - they seemed tired. Masterda saw them and asked Naresh - "Why are you completely silent? What happened to you?"

Naresh said - "Nothing has happened. We are all physically healthy; but we have come back unsatisfied."

Masterda was confused and asked - "Naresh, if you came back disabled? I do not understand. Tell me what happened?"

Naresh said - "We went to the club-house as planned. We hurriedly entered the club-house through various doors and windows - but surprise! The hall was completely empty! The gentle men had all gone home by eight or nine."

Masterda said, "Don't be upset about that. Chittagong city is under our control, we will take revenge."

After all the attacks that day, they chased them into the jungle in the darkness of night, taking refuge in the Jalalabad hills as they went. And four days passed there.

The revolutionaries knew that the British forces would come looking for them. So everyone was on their own responsibility. Everyone was ready with their rifles. Naresh saw a man coming this way, the news went to Ananta Singh and said - "A man is coming this way pretending to be crazy; we have handcuffed him. It seems that he is a policeman in white - what should we do with him?"

Ananta said, "Let's go and see who he is." Seeing him, he looked like a policeman. Still, Ananta didn't want to punish him. "Let him stay. If you find his identity, release him." The man didn't give any identity and didn't release him either.

The day was April 22, 1930, the armed British forces arrived in the Jalalabad hills. After this, a fierce battle began, the battle continued, then stopped for a while. When the battle began again for the second time, they won. Then the third battle began, the battle reached a terrible state.

British machine gun fire came and penetrated Vidhu's heart. The gun slipped from his hand. The body twitched and became still. Before Bidhu breathed her last, she said to Naresh Roy - 'Naresh, come... you too... receive you!' - (Naresh, I am going - you come - I will welcome you)."

Bidhu Bhattacharya bid Naresh farewell in the Jalalabad hills, and said that he would be waiting to welcome Naresh. So perhaps Naresh could no longer ignore his friend's longing. He held the rifle tightly in his hand and kept firing. He wanted revenge for the blood of his friend, the blood of the enemy. Machine gun bullets were coming at the speed of the wind, he had no regard for his own self-defense. The death of a friend must be avenged.

Every now and then, Naresh raises his head and aims the machine gun at them, firing! At that time the machine gun shot came and went out through his chest. Immediately, he fell to the ground with his rifle in his hand - and in an instant, he said goodbye forever. As if he has to go somewhere very quickly, the invitation of his friend Bidhu that must be saved.

Naresh Roy and Vidhu Bhattacharya were very close friends. They passed their medical exams at the same time. They lived in the same mess. They died at the same time on the Jalalabad battlefield.

Ganesh Ghosh

Bidhu Bhushan Bhattacharya (Bidhu)

On 18 April 1930, Bidhu Bhushan Bhattacharya participated in the revolutionary activities during the attack on the Chittagong Arsenal. He was one of the victorious forces in the Battle of Jalalabad Hills. He died on the battlefield after being shot.

Bidhu Bhushan Bhattacharya was born in Lesiara, Brahmanbaria district. He was the son of a lower middle-class family. He was a classmate and the same age as Naresh Roy, one of the revolutionaries of the Chittagong Youth Uprising. After passing his matriculation, Bidhu Bhushan went from Comilla to Chittagong to study medicine. He had the revolutionary Naresh Roy as a classmate in that medical school. From his childhood, he had to struggle with poverty and study.

Many times, Bidhu could not afford the food of his boarding house. He used to satisfy his hunger by eating the lowest standard food of the cheap hotels. But the oppression of his poverty could never burden his smiling and confident mind. "Don't care" was his motto in life.

He always made people laugh with his words. There was never any boredom in his humor. His store of humor was always rich with new elements.

He was also exceptionally skilled in physical exercise. His strong, fit physique was the envy of the club members. He was one of the best boxers in Chittagong. Bidhu was unique in bringing the Mastans under his control, the Mastans of the city feared him like Yama.

With the help of his classmate Naresh Roy, he joined the revolutionary group. Responding to the Masterdar's call, the addiction to destruction entered his blood.

Bidhu Bhattacharya passed his medical degree with a gold medal, but he could no longer serve the common people. He heard from his master - "The British rulers have blocked the path to the welfare of our country." The common youth of Chittagong used to say that Bidhu Bhushan Bhattacharya and Naresh Roy were the right and left hands of Ganesh Ghosh and Anantaa Singh. Bidhu Bhattacharya's efficiency was also extraordinary.

In 1930, revolutionary Tarkeshwar Dastidar was seriously injured while preparing explosives at the Chittagong Congress office. To hide him from the city to the village, Bidhu Bhattacharya of the Medical College, Naresh Roy, Jatin Das of Mahira village and Sushil De of Dhorla village took Tarkeshwar to Kheyaghat. To raise Tarakeswar to Sampan. Before reaching the Kheaghat, a group of local people blocked the road. They became suspicious when they saw Tarakeswar in a bandage. Seeing that Bidhu Bhattacharya, Naresh Roy and the revolutionaries were late in returning, Ananta Singh and Ganesh Ghosh came to see him. Seeing the crowd, Ananta and Ganesh shouted loudly - "Kan hai?" Immediately, the people blocking the way fled in fear. Then Tarakeshwar was lifted into the sampan.

Now, the attack on the Chittagong armory has begun at the call of Masterda Surya Sen. Various plans are being made for the attack. Attack ok, but want two cars. They want to keep the car under their control for three hours by rendering the driver unconscious with chloroform. They have given the responsibility of testing this chloroform to Bidhu Bhattacharya and Naresh Roy, 'Gold Medalist' students of the Medical College.

On 18th April 1930, Bidhubhushan would be present at the police line attack. That day, the rifle-bearing guards were walking silently. There was a guard room next to it where the rest of the soldiers were resting or sleeping. The second group led by Ganesh Ghosh, Ananta Singh, Bidhu Bhattacharya, Haripada Mahajan, Saroj Guha and Himanshu Sen arrived in a car and stopped at the police line.

It was about ten o'clock at night. Three arms' length away from the guard, the pistols of Ananta Singh and Ganesh Ghosh roared together. Immediately, the guard fell to the ground trembling like an uprooted tree. As soon as the guard was shot, everyone shouted 'Inclab Zindabad', 'Death to imperialism', 'Long live the revolution' and everyone started firing, so that no guard could pick up the rifle.

That day, they broke down the door of the armory and took possession of the police line along with rifles, revolvers, and cartridges. The British Union Jack was found and burned as Masterda said.

This time, the national flag was raised in the joy of victory. The guns were fired three times in the open sky and saluted. Then, in the darkness of the night, they went out in search of safe shelter. Finally, they went to the Jalalabad hills and took shelter. They spent four days in the Jalalabad hills, hungry and thirsty.

April 22, 1930. Armed British forces arrived at the foot of the Jalalabad hills. War was inevitable, word of mouth had spread. They checked their respective guns and revolvers - whether the trigger, striking and chamber were loaded.

War is inevitable, the shadow of death is all around. Everyone understood that the ultimate moment of testing had arrived. However, everyone's laughter and laughter did not go away. Nirmal Sen said - 'Ambikada, today may have to die.' But before I die, I want to eat chop cutlets.' Ambika Chakraborty smiled and said - 'The young comrades are counting down the time with the desire for war. "Those who have a strong hunger for armed struggle, will they want to eat chop cutlets now?" As Ambika Chakraborty finished speaking, the already gold medal winning doctor Bidhu Bhattacharya burst out laughing and said - "What are you saying Ambikada? You are only talking about seeing chariots, we will see chariots, we will sell bananas - we will also fight, and we will also eat chop cutlets.

The revolutionaries are spread out on the hills in different groups. The historic battle on the Jalalabad hills has begun. On one side, the British forces are raining bullets and rifles, on the other, the revolutionaries are raining bullets. Suddenly, three or four bullets hit the Bidhu at the same time. Despite being shot, Lokenath, who was standing next to him, said to Bal: - 'Lokada! Lokada! after all this time the bullet hit me). What a surprise! He has been waiting so long for a bullet to hit him. The bullet had hit him, so Anand told Lokenath Bal the news. A few more bullets hit Bidhu. Perhaps Bidhu being a doctor, was hesitating to let the rifle bullet pierce his chest.

One after another, bullets hit Bidhu Bhushan Bhattacharya, then Bidhu said to himself - 'Hey! How many more bullets will be needed? When Lagbi, then why around? Why not hit it straight in the chest?

If there had been time, he might have said more. But never got that chance again, British machine gun fire came and penetrated Bidhu's heart. The gun fell from his hand. The body twitched and became still. Before taking his last breath, Bidhu addressed Naresh Roy and said- b'I am going, Naresh. "You come - I will welcome you."

Lokenath Bal was a witness to all these events, he was nearby. Lokenath was overwhelmed by what he said. Bidhu, who was shot in the Jalalabad hills, is counting his last hours in a wounded state. Even then he left forever laughing and joking with his friends.

Jiten Dasgupta

The young revolutionary youth of Bengal had a truly extraordinary talent. They appeared on the battlefield at a very young age with pistols in their hands. They stood with their chests held high in front of the British army, it seemed that they were born to defend the motherland. In the end, will be reborn to see the face of a new sun by sacrificing your life on the battlefield. The rising of a new sun means the freedom of the motherland. This freedom is yours, mine, and all of us. Today, the person I will talk about here is Jiten Dasgupta. He participated in the battle of Jalalabad and died.

No specific information was found about Jiten Dasgupta. However, I have tried to present the information that was found.

Jiten Dasgupta was born in the village of Gairla in Chittagong. He lived in Rangoon, where he studied at the Bengal Academy. Then he returned to Chittagong from Rangoon a few days before the attack on the Chittagong armoury. Within a few days, he came into contact with the Chittagong Revolutionary Party. Gradually, the revolutionary party's relationship with him began to grow closer.

Later, when he came into close contact with the revolutionary party, he joined the revolutionary party of Chittagong. Due to his enthusiasm and activities, he became a trusted worker of the revolutionary members. Within a few days, it was decided to attack the armory of Chittagong. The date was fixed for 18 April 1930. When they were in financial trouble, like everyone else, Jiten Dasgupta also extended a helping hand.

Finally, on the historic day of April 18, he went out fully equipped to open a new chapter in history. During the attack on the Chittagong Armory, he participated in the attack on the police line on the orders of the Masterdar. That day, they broke the door of the armory and took possession of the police line along with rifles, revolvers and cartridges. As the Masterdar had said, the British Union Jack was found and burned. There the revolutionaries had to engage in light war.

This time, the national flag was raised in the joy of victory. The guns were fired three times in the open sky and saluted. Then they left in the darkness of the night. Despite the darkness all around, their eyes crossed the mountains and forests and finally took refuge in the Jalalabad hills. Four days passed in Jalalabad, everyone almost fell ill from hunger and thirst for water.

That day was April 22nd. The revolutionaries took up position on the top of the Jalalabad hill. A group of British soldiers appeared under the hill. A terrible war began between them. They were in constant battle with the British armed forces. At one time, one revolutionary soldier after another was losing his life to the bullets of the British soldiers. Yet he has no regrets. Suddenly a bunch of shots came Half of Jiten Dasgupta's flesh, including his skull, disappeared. Within moments, Jiten's eyelids closed. His life's lamp went out. He died in the battle of Jalalabad leaving his blood signature.

The land of Jalalabad is blessed with the blood of this brave revolutionary. For this, we can also proudly say, we are proud, we are Bengalis. Long live Bangla.

Motilal Kanungo (Moti)

The blood of martyrs will not be in vain. The freedom struggle is a great struggle for which hundreds of young people sacrificed their lives. They had to leave their homes and families for the sake of the country. Some lost their sons, some lost their husbands and some lost their fathers. Motherland India was blessed with the blood of these martyrs. Let's listen to something about the revolutionary Motilal Kanungo. Who fought like a hero in the historic campaign of Jalalabad hills and died.

Motilal Kanungo was born in 1913 in Kanungo Para, Chittagong. His father's name was Durga Mohan Kanungo. Motilal Kanungo and Ananda Prasad Gupta (Ananda Prasad Gupta was one of the revolutionaries of the Chittagong Youth Uprising) studied at the same time in the Collegiate School. Motilal Kanungo was quite good in studies, but the family's poverty and hardships were not very good for them. His father Durga Mohan Kanungo was a renowned homeopathic doctor.

Motilal Kanungo lived in Kautala Para, Nandakanan area of Chittagong city. He took the matriculation examination in 1930, accompanied by revolutionary Ananda Prasad Gupta. Then he joined the revolutionary party, devoted his heart and soul to the cause of revolution. He always thought about how to become a successful revolutionary. How to establish a new India. The welfare of the country is never possible while there is political slavery. There is no work to make the revolution successful that Motilal Kanungo could not do. He did everything effortlessly.

Masterda ordered Motilal to learn how to aim a gun, but where could he get one? At that time, it was a legal offense for them to have a gun in a conquered country. He thought about his neighbor Mihir Basu's father, Ashubodh Basu, a high-ranking government official. He has a gun, so he befriends Mihir Bose. And Motilal developed a very beautiful relationship with Mihir

Bose. Motilal also called on Mihir Basu to join the revolution, and finally Motilal's hopes were fulfilled. Mihir Bose and Motilal along with a few others used to secretly take the gun of Mihir Bose's father and train in the afternoon.

At Motilal's urging, Mihir Basu became a very good revolutionary devotee. Mihir can do anything for the welfare of the country. But if we want to strengthen this revolution, we want weapons, ammunition and money. But where can he get all this? Now everyone including Masterda Surya Sen started planning. Let us take away the wealth of our country from those who have looted it. In the end it was decided to attack the armory of Chittagong.

Then came the day, April 18, 1930, when Moti and Mihir Bose joined the attack on the Chittagong armoury. The day before, on April 17, Mihir had also stolen his father's gun and brought it to the revolutionary group. Motilal participated in the attack on the police line during the attack on the Chittagong armoury. That day, they broke down the door of the armoury and took possession of the police line along with rifles, revolvers and cartridges. As the master had said, they found the British Union Jack and set it on fire.

This time the national flag was hoisted in celebration of victory. The guns were fired three times in the open sky and saluted. Then, in the darkness of the night, they went out in search of safe shelter. Finally, they went to the Jalalabad hills and took shelter. He spent four days in the mountains of Jalalabad in hunger and thirst.

That day was April 22nd. Motilal fought like a hero in every battle in the Jalalabad hills. He was seriously injured in that battle and lost consciousness. The revolutionaries won the first battle. Later, the police attacked again. A fierce battle ensued, Machine gun bullets hit Ambika Chakraborty. She gave her life on the battlefield. As soon as the revolutionaries got gold, their voices thundered - we want revenge, we want revenge. The guns in the hands of the revolutionaries seemed to become more powerful.

The firing is continuous - no one pays any attention, no care - want the destruction of the enemy. Machine gun fire is hitting back. A number of bullets hit Motilal, who fell to the ground. He could not say anything. Only the murmur of could be heard. His lips were quivering, as if he was asking for water. Subodh Roy was a little distance away, he looked at Moti, Moti was asking for water. But how can water be given to him? Going to give him water means stepping into the face of death. But Moti must be given water. Subodh rubbed his chest and took the water carrier to Moti. The water jug was almost empty, and the remaining two or three drops of water were not enough to quench Moti's thirst.

Moti could not recognize who had given him water. He could not even say anything. Subodh gave water and went back to his place. The next morning, April 23rd, he was shouting for water, but the barbaric British army did not even give Motilal the opportunity to be a prisoner of war. British officers, doctors and the Indian army were present there, they found Moti alive. He was still breathing, Dr. Weldon Sahib examined him and found that there was no way for Moti to survive. He did not think it was necessary to send him to the hospital. So Weldon Sahib injected him with morphine and left him there.

Moti's heart had not yet stopped working, Before it stopped, he was thrown into the burning fire, As much as there was hope to survive. That too was over. Motilal was burned alive on a burning pyre. The life of Moti Kanungo in the Battle of Jalalabad ended.

Ardhendu Dastidar

Ardhendu Dastidar is one of the martyrs of Jalalabad hill battle. He joined the revolutionary activities by responding to the call of Masterda Surya Sen. He was born in 1911 in a middle-class family in Dhalghat, Chittagong. His father's name was Chandrakumar Dastidar. The three brothers were actively involved in the same armed revolutionary movement. The elder brother's name was Purnendu Dastidar, a personality involved in the Chittagong Rebellion, and the younger brother Sukhendu Dastidar was the youngest revolutionary of the Chittagong Youth Rebellion.

In 1925, Ardhendu Dastidar joined the revolutionary party. When Masterda Suryasen was in prison, Ardhendu continued the work of the organization with a few workers. He was a simple worker, for which Masterda Suryasen loved him very much. When asked to give an example of an ideal intelligent revolutionary worker, Masterda Suryasen would mention the name of Ardhendu Dastidar.

Ardhendu Dastidar's father was a non-violent patriot, opposed to his association with revolutionaries. Because of this, Ardhendu had to endure a lot of torture at home. At the end, Ardhendu thought and saw that if he wanted to continue on the path of revolution, he would have to leave his home. In the end he did so, thus the separation of father and son took place forever. After that, he lived in the Congress office near Masterda Surya Sen.

After that, he studied at a homeopathy school for some time. Later, due to financial problems, he had to leave his studies. From then on, he spent all his time working for the organization as a general worker.

From a young age, Ardhendu was always a philanthropist. He first gained fame in the field of public service as a volunteer of the Ramakrishna Ashram. In 1926, he went to the devastated Mirzapur on behalf of the Ramakrishna Ashram to take charge of relief. Before the Chittagong Armory attack, while making the bomb, the bomb exploded and Ardhendu was seriously injured and several parts of his body were burnt.

The flesh of the body droops. Even bones of the body can be seen in places. Fearing that the incident would become known, he hid all his pain in just aha and uh, and suffered all the hardships. The police could not guess even a single detail of this incident. As soon as his body recovered from the wound, he again jumped into the youth rebellion.

The body is sick, meanwhile on April 18, according to the Masterdar's instructions, the Chittagong arsenal must be attacked. The revolutionaries tried to convince him that he shouldn't go to the attack with this sick body, but he listened to everyone and eventually decided to join in.

Despite his physical illness, Ardhendu participated in the attack on the police line. That day, they broke down the door of the armory and took possession of the police line along with rifles, revolvers and cartridges. The British Union Jack was found and burned as Masterda said.

This time the national flag was hoisted in celebration of victory. The guns were fired three times in the open sky and saluted. Then, in the darkness of the night, they went out in search of safe shelter. Finally, they went to the Jalalabad hills and took shelter. He spent four days in the mountains of Jalalabad in hunger and thirst.

That day was April 22nd. The British army rushed in, and within a moment the machine gun fire started raining down on one side and the rifle fire of the revolutionaries on the other. Their position was very weak. Still, Ardhendu is dealing with the enemy like a warrior. A hero has no fear of death, so he went into the battle of killing the enemy without paying attention to himself.

Suddenly, a barrage of machine gun bullets came and ripped through Ardhendu's lower abdomen. He has been seriously injured. His wound seemed to be more serious. Despite being wounded, he fired in response to every shot fired by the enemy. Sometimes he raises the rifle and fires. He did not give up until the war was over.

At the end of the war, the revolutionaries thought Ardhendu was dead and left him there. Apart from Ardhendu, Ambika Chakraborty and Moti Kanungo were alive in injured condition there. When Ambika Chakraborty regained consciousness, she heard someone's voice. She thought that everyone except the dead comrades had gone with Masterdar. Whose voice was it? But was anyone still alive? Then she heard Ardhendu's voice, - "Ambikada, are you alive?"

- Yes, yes, I'm alive. Where are you? How are you? Can you get up somehow? Try it - slowly we will go down from the hill. Seeing Ambika Chakraborty, Ardhendu seemed to regain his strength. He got up very forcefully. He couldn't find where he put the revolver.

Ardhendu could not stand properly due to the bullet in his lower abdomen. He somehow managed to stand bent over with his weight on the barrel of the gun. Then Ardhendu and Ambika Chakraborty started walking towards the northeast of the hill. About fifteen minutes passed in just ten to twelve yards. Ardhhendu could no longer walk on the north side of the hill. He had no strength left in his body to walk. He fell on his knees there. Ambika told Chakraborty - "Ambika, I can't walk anymore, I don't have the strength to walk anymore. You keep moving forward. You have to survive. Now, if you look at Sentiment in a big way, you won't be late thinking about me. Tell Masterda that I kept his word - "Liberty or death!"

Ambika Chakraborty said to Ardhendu - "Brother, I will definitely tell Masterda about you. May you live long, may Biplob live long." Ambika Chakraborty left after saying this.

The next morning, April 23, British officers and doctors and Indian troops were present there. Ardhendu Dastidar was found almost dead in a bush on the northeast side of the hill. Doctor Weldon gave first aid and sent him to the city hospital. Ardhendu was kept under strict police guard.

The account of the Government Civil Surgeon Dr. Ghosh shows that on April 22nd, in Jalalabad, the lower part of the spine of Ardhendu Dastidar was broken by a bullet. Two of his ribs were also broken. The day was April 23, 1930, but he was still unable to die peacefully on his deathbed.

A deputy magistrate kept asking him one question after another. But he did not yield to the English until his death. Despite asking question after question, the overzealous magistrate could not extract a single word or even the slightest acknowledgement from him.

The Assistant Civil Surgeon Dr. Ghosh came to testify in the 'Armory Looting' case. The best identification of the revolutionary character of Shaheed Ardhendu emerged through the description he gave. Here the most significant part of that description is mentioned exactly:- "When Ardhendu was admitted he was dying and I, therefore, sent the requistion to the Magistrate as a matter of course...I was present by the side of the patient all the time the Deputy Magistrate was there. The Magistrate asked where his village home was and Ardhendu declined to answer. When the Dy. Magistrate questioned him he said "Amar hat tat dhare asche" He was in a bad condition- his pulse clearly and was fully conscious. I understood that he declined to make any statement inspite of the repeated questions of the Magistrate." The revolutionary Ardhendu died keeping the honor of a true revolutionary intact.

When questioned about whether the magistrate's harassment had hastened Ardhendu's death, Dr. Ghosh replied in a roundabout way: "If he had been my private patient, I would not have allowed any interference with him." Ardhendu was only 19 years old at the time of his death.

Ardhendu was an ideal character of revolutionary India. He achieved glory for his bravery in the Battle of Jalalabad.

Amarendra Nandi

It is truly unbelievable that the young men of Bengal jumped into the freedom struggle at such a young age. Today I will talk about one such young man, who also displayed his bravery in the Jalalabad hills. His name was Amarendra Nandi, he was born in Chittagong around 1913. His father's name was Rasiklal Nandi. He used to take up public work from his childhood, and his extraordinary interest in it was evident.

While living in the village, he became known as a public servant, winning the hearts of everyone as an idealistic young man. He was born into a middle-class family. At one time, Amarendra Nandi took the vows of a monk, left home and family and went to Jagadbandhu Ashram in Chittagong for shelter. From there, his new life of studies began. After that, he came to Sadarghat Club and got admitted.

Many revolutionaries tried hard to bring this idealistic young man to their team, but in the end they were disappointed. Since joining the club, Amarendra has shown no interest in anything except physical exercise.

His use seems to deliberately avoid the political activities of the revolutionaries. Amarendra thought about it and decided that there was no place for revolution in the work of public service that he was engaged in. Gradually, this wall of his thinking began to break, and a new change in his life was seen. He saw that the revolutionary members of the Sadarghat Club, who were just as idealistic and devoted as he were, had also embarked on public service. But their ideology was different, they wanted to do public service through revolution.

In any case, the British rule must be removed from the country, that will be the work of public service. The people of the country must be rescued from the clutches of the British. All-round public development is not possible until the state power of the country comes into the hands of true patriots.

During the Chittagong Rebellion, he was an intermediate student of Chittagong College. One day, surprising everyone, Amarendra joined the revolutionary party. He proved in a few days that he was also an idealistic and revolutionary. On 18 April 1930, on the orders of Masterda Surya Sen, the Chittagong Arsenal was attacked. Finally, they went to the Jalalabad hills and took refuge. On the night of 18 April, he participated in the attack on the police line. Due to his extraordinary skills, Masterda sent him from Jalalabad to the city.

Ananta Singh and Ganesh Ghosh were in the city at that time, there was no contact with them. So some people were sent, but they did not return. On April 21st, Masterda, Ambika Chakraborty and Nirmal Sen decided to make a last attempt. This time they would select two people and send them together.

The revolutionaries were resting in small groups on the hill. Masterda and Nirmal Sen went to each of them and said - "We want two people who will not return saying 'I couldn't'. We must establish contact with Anant Singh, Ganesh Ghosh and Jiban Ghoshal." But no one said no, everyone agreed. Everyone was ready to go. Among them all, Masterda selected Amarendra Nandi and one more. Amarendra was told to return by half past six or seven. Amarendra Nandi and his other companion bid farewell to everyone and proceeded to fulfill their great responsibility. All the friends gave their revolutionary greetings and they too, greeting everyone, went down the hill.

The military is then patrolling all over the city, setting up camps in suspicious locations. Amarendra broke through all their cordons and entered the city. but it was just right, but having covered thirteen or fourteen miles between eight and nine hours, it was impossible to return so far by seven o'clock, in search of the rest.

The day was April 24th, in the morning, Constable Chandrakumar Dey saw Amarendra Nandi in the empty house of J. M. Sengupta on Sadarghat Road with a pistol in both hands. He immediately ran and informed the police superintendent at Sadarghat police station. Mr. Johnson was given the responsibility of arresting Amarendra Nandi, he appeared at that house with all the soldiers, the house was surrounded from all sides. They searched a few houses nearby, but no one was found there. Amarendra was in a small room downstairs in that house. After a while, he was found there. Amarendra was hiding in a khaki dress, dhoti, bed sheet and a green belt.

Then the fierce firing began. On one side, countless military personnel and on the other side, Amarendra alone. Who is called the brave boy Abhimanyu surrounded by seven chariots. The gunfire of the revolver did not stop for a moment. Amarendra, holding a revolver loaded with bullets in both hands, was responding to the gunfire equally.

Amarendra finally took shelter under a culvert. Amarendra was seriously injured. He was repeatedly asked to surrender. But he did not do so. He tried to escape by breaking through the military cordon and failed. He would not surrender either, instead he thought it better to execute himself. He sacrificed himself like a hero, yet he did not bow his head to the British imperialist ruler. Finally, the culvert was broken, he was rescued in his injured state, and a doctor named Jagada Biswas gave him first aid. After that, he was sent to the hospital. Amarendra Nandi died there on 24th April 1930.

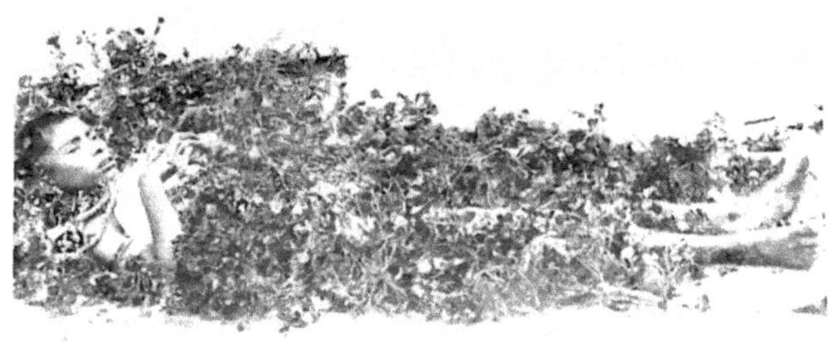

The next morning, Amarendra's body was postmortem. I quote the relevant part from the official statement on this matter exactly: "...next morning a post mortem examination was made by the Civil Surgeon who found the following injuries on his body: (1) an elliptical punctured wound with blackended edges just under the chin-this was the entrance wound. (2) A stellate perforating wound on the top of the head about one inch above the hair margin-this was the exit wound. The bullet had passed through the base of the tongue, the brain and the skull. (3) A circular punctured wound with blackened edges on the chest. From the position of the wound on the top of the head and the fact that the margins of the wounds under the chin and on the chest were blackened, the Civil Surgeon was of opinion that the wounds were suicidal, that in all probability Amarendra had a hot himself first on the chest and finding he was not dying quickly enough, had shot himself again through the head."

Kalarpole Clash

The battle of Jalalabad Hill is also over. In the darkness of the night, the revolutionaries descended from the hill and scattered to one place after another. They spent a few days here and there. Then everyone gathered together again. Again, a new attack plan was planned. This time, the Masterdar ordered that the European Club at the foot of the hill must be attacked.

The Jalalabad hills were stained with the blood of revolutionaries. Now, it was time to take revenge, and a few reckless young men came forward. Among them were - Rajat Sen, Deboprasad Gupta, Manoranjan Sen, Swadesh Roy, Subodh Chowdhury and Fanindra Nandi.

On May 5, 1930, six young men armed with weapons set out. The Pahartali European Club is located a short distance from the Ballentine Ghat on the Karnaphuli River. The club is very secure. As soon as evening falls, the British gentlemen and ladies get into a frenzy. At that time, there was tight security around the city. Since there was tight security, they returned, waiting for the right time.

Now they will return to their secret hideout. They will cross the Karnaphuli River on the road to Firingi bazar and go to Rajat's house. Rajat's house was in Firingi bazar. Rajat's mother Binodini Devi was the mother of all revolutionaries. Binodini Devi loved everyone very much. They were hungry and would also eat food from their mother's hand. One of them came and said - "Auntie, I am very hungry."

Binodini Devi said - "Giving, Father, sit down for a while, I will arrange it right away." Dinner is not done? Rajat's younger brother came running and informed - "Dada, the police is coming." Everyone bowed to Maasima and left through the back door in the darkness of the night. Karnaphuli ran towards the river, leaving the plate of food, then jumped into a sampan. As the revolutionaries said, the boatman was steering the sampan with all his might.

The police force, led by Khan Bahadur Asanullah, chased after them. The police force repeatedly said - "Stop the sampan." But the sampan did not stop. As soon as the sampan reached the river, the revolutionaries jumped off and disappeared. When the police force arrived, they saw that the revolutionaries had disappeared. So they spread the news among the villagers - "There are robbers in the village, if you can catch them, there will be a big reward."

This time the revolutionaries had to face a strong obstacle. The revolutionaries and the villagers engaged in a pitched battle. A villager targeted Deboprasad and hit him with his fist. Deboprasad survived for a short while, but his right arm was almost severed from his shoulder. What a terrible pain. Still, his morale was strong, his arm continued to hang loose.

The revolutionaries started firing back at the villagers. Some of the villagers fell down. The revolutionaries shouted repeatedly - "We are not robbers, we are Swadeshi. The British are our enemies. Don't stop us." However, the villagers did not believe them. They did not give up on the revolutionaries for the reward.

It was dark all around, and the roads and ghats were unknown to them. Fanindra Nandi got lost in the darkness and was caught by the police the next morning.

The five revolutionaries came to a stop on the Kalarpole Bridge while running. On the other side of the bridge was a police post, behind them were villagers. There was no way out, Subodh Chowdhury was caught while trying to escape from the police.

The remaining four, Deboprasad Gupta, Rajat Sen, Manoranjan Sen and Swadesh Roy, entered the village of Julda. It was almost dawn. They were passing by a house, and suddenly seeing an old woman, the revolutionaries asked her for some rice. The mother's heart was filled with compassion. The old woman said - "You take shelter in that forest. I am bringing you some rice." The householder brought some panta rice and curry and said - 'I will arrange for you to fill your stomachs with food later.'

The sun was appearing in the eastern sky, turning blood red, i.e. on May 6, while the police force began a combing search. A villager named Ahmad Miah, seeing the revolutionaries in the forest, shouted, "They are hiding there." As soon as he heard this, a group of police forces led by D. I. G. Farmer surrounded the area. Seeing the police force approaching, the pistols in the hands of the revolutionaries roared together.

The armed struggle of the Kalarpole began. Heavy firing continued on both sides. After firing for some time, the police officers were unable to move forward due to fear. On the orders of D. I. G. Farmer, the head inspector took the microphone and said - "Drop your weapons and surrender. The only meaning of fighting like this is death."

Manoranjan replied - Manoranjan does not know - how to surrender? Manoranjan does not know how to surrender. I, want to Jatin Mukherjee of Balasore. I will fight like Jatin Mukherjee. Another person was heard saying - "We will not let ourselves be captured as long as we live." The voice of the other companion was heard - "No, no, certainly not. We will die, but we will not let ourselves be captured."

The gunfire started again from Saravan. How long will the four pistols fight against the large police force? The bullets are almost gone. Swadesh Roy fell to the ground under the bullets. Rajat now said to Manoranjan - "Mana! Swadesh has just died. Debu will not survive, it is better to surrender than to surrender. I am shooting Debu, you will shoot me, understand?"

Immediately after saying this, Rajat shot to end Debu's suffering. Manoranjan shot friend Rajat twice. After that he shot the last two shots in his chest. Swadesh Roy, Manoranjan Sen and Rajat Sen said goodbye forever. However, the battlefield of Sharaban in Zulda village was not finished. Deboprasad Gupta still had life left in his body, he was having a hard time breathing. At that moment, the head inspector came running and said, "The elder is here, do you want to say something?" Deboprasad replied in a loud voice - "Who is the big man, Lowman, Lowman, I have both hands immobile, otherwise I would have shot him right away."

Saying these words, Deboprasad Gupta breathed his last.

Deboprasad Gupta, Rajat Sen, Manoranjan Sen

& Swadesh Roy

Rajat Sen

Rajat Sen was born in 1913 in Chittagong. His father's name was Ranjanlal Sen and his mother's name was Binodini Devi. Rajat Sen was good at everything from sports to writing and reading since childhood. No one ever saw him sitting still. He would captivate everyone with his boundless energy. He was proficient in horse riding and driving a motor car. Rajat Sen was one of the best football players from Chittagong.

As a child, Rajat was the school's ideal boy scout while studying in a collegiate school. When Rajat Sen was a student of class 10, the Lat Saheb of Bengal, Stanley Jackson, came to visit their Collegiate School. At that time, Rajat sketched a pencil portrait of him in front of Lat Saheb in just two minutes and presented it to him. Lat Saheb granted Rajat a scholarship for his art studies and promised that if Rajat gets admission in Calcutta Art College one day, he will extend all kinds of help to him. Thus, Rajat also got the status of an artist.

At one point, he joined Masterda Surya Sen's Indian Republican Army. In 1930, Masterda started planning to attack the Chittagong armory. But it was not possible to fight with bare hands! So everyone was told that as much money as possible would come forward to help. Suddenly one day what Rajat did, he brought many expensive ornaments and some seals from home. Rajat came and said, "I have emptied everything that was inside the Sindhuk."

On 18th April, Rajat Sen joined the Chittagong Youth Rebellion. He took part in the attack on the Auxiliary Force Armoury on the orders of the Masterdar. Around ten o'clock in the night, Loknath Ball's car arrived and entered the A.F.I headquarters compound. Headquarters. Coming along this road, leaving Sergeant Ferrell's quarters on the left, the vehicle turned right and stopped in front of the Armoury.

The steering wheel of the car was in the hands of Makhan Ghoshal. Also in the car were Loknath Bal, Nirmal Sen, Rajat Sen, Subodh Choudhury and Fanindra Nandi. Two soldiers got out of the car and walked behind General Loknath Bal in the posture of a bodyguard. Looking at Loknath's clothes, he looks like an officer. The three of them started climbing the steps of the balcony, a sentry officer saluted Loknath in error.

As soon as the salute was given, Loknath's pistol roared. On receiving the signal to fire, Rajat Sen and Nirmal Sen fired, and the sentry fell to the ground. The other sepoys ran away wherever they could. Through the lonely darkness, ten people shouted together - "Bandemataram - Inclub Zindabad."

After attacking the armory, they set out along the mountain road in search of safe shelter. Rajat is first, everyone follows behind him. Rajat leads the way, cutting through the jungle and bushes ahead.

(The rest of it is on pages 54 to 57)

Manoranjan Sen (Mana)

Manoranjan Sen, he was born on May 6, 1913 in the Burma region of Chittagong. His father's name was Rajnikant Sen. He was the son of a very poor family. He studied in Intermediate at Chittagong College. His revolutionary spirit began while he was a student. He came in contact with the revolutionary party at a very young age. He joined the revolutionary party. Then he used to participate in stick games and chess games.

The extent of poverty that Manoranjan had to endure could never be understood by looking at his face. He always had a smile on his face. Once, an intelligence officer of the Chittagong Division set out to collect secret information from the revolutionary party. He was very enthusiastically looking for a member of the party who would give the intelligence officer information about the revolutionary party for money.

The intelligence officer caught sight of Manoranjan. Living in extreme poverty, he would surely be trapped in a money trap. One day, taking this opportunity to talk to Manoranjan, he raised his proposal. He made the proposal with great hopes but received an angry rejection from Manoranjan.

On 18 April 1930, Manoranjan joined the Chittagong Armory attack. He was a first year student of the Intermediate of Chittagong College at that time. On the day of the Chittagong Armory attack, he took part with the police line attackers. Later, on 22 April, he also participated in the Battle of Jalalabad Hills.

(The rest of it is on pages 54 to 57)

Ambika Chakraborty

Deboprasad Gupta (Debu)

Deboprasad Gupta, was born in Dhaka in 1911. His father's name was Yogendranath Gupta. Ananda Prasad Gupta, one of the revolutionaries of the Chittagong Arsenal attack, was three years younger than his own younger brother, Debu. They were in Chittagong from their childhood. From his school days, Deboprasad Gupta earned the reputation of a student among his teachers.

He passed his matriculation with distinction in 1928, then joined college as a science student. That year he came in contact with the revolutionary party. That same year, he accompanied the delegates to the Calcutta Congress session along with Masterda and other revolutionaries and attended the Deboprasad Gupta session. He spent a few days of the session in the delegate camp.

Then Deboprasad Gupta left Kolkata for Chittagong with great enthusiasm. He devoted himself fully to the work of the party. He attracted everyone's attention because of his great courage.

He was never afraid of anyone. He would not remain silent until the work assigned to him by the party was completely solved.

It was a few months before the Chittagong armory attack. With the annual college exams just around the corner, his family members were constantly telling him to prepare well for the exams. Debprasad decided since then and what will happen with the test? After a few days the call will come to jump into a great sacrifice. By the time his test results are out, he may no longer exist in the world. So what is the use of memorizing reading books?

Everyone is worried that Debu has never done this in his student life. But why is he neglecting his studies now during this important time of the exam? But during the exam, he sat in the exam hall to take the exam, However, instead of writing the answers to the questions in the exam notebook, he filled the notebook with pictures. The professor who was in the exam room was surprised to see - What strange pictures instead of answers to questions in the exam booklet of such a good and talented student.

The news slowly spread from mouth to mouth. It even reached the revolutionary leaders. When asked if the news was true, Debu said with a smile - "When the test results come out, I won't be in this world anymore - "So passing the exam or failing it is the same for me."

Then on 18 April 1930, he participated in the attack on the Chittagong Arsenal. Then on 22 April, he joined the Battle of Jalalabad Hills.

(The rest of it is on pages 54 to 57)

Swadesh Ranjan Roy (Swadesh)

Swadesh Roy, one of the revolutionaries of the Kalarpole clash. But some of the incidents in his revolutionary life are very painful. Most of the revolutionaries were his friends, but no one gave him a place in the revolutionary party. Swadesh Roy was the son of a wealthy family. He was brought up in a comfortable environment. Like everyone else, he used to go to the Sadarghat exercise club. There he developed friendships with Ananda Prasad Gupta and other revolutionaries.

Swadesh Roy, who had grown up in luxury, might not be able to withstand the harshness of the revolutionaries. Therefore, the revolutionary leaders did not invite him to any conspiratorial activities. The leaders had instructions for Swadesh Roy's revolutionary friends of the same age not to involve him in adventurous activities.

Swadesh realized that his friends were about to do something adventurous, and he also realized that his friends were deliberately pushing him away. They were not inviting him to their political activities.

April 18, 1930, about three hours before the Chittagong armory attack. The revolutionaries are all waiting in a room for Himanshu, Himanshu has gone to collect the car. Haripada Mahajan was guarding the door of the room. Swadesh Roy suddenly entered the room without permission and without any hindrance. Everyone was shocked by this. He was not a member of this secret organization. Deboprasad was a close friend of his.

A few months ago, however, Naresh Roy had told Ananta to experiment with Swadesh together. But he did not do so. The party had stopped accepting new members as a matter of principle six months before the attack. Therefore, the revolutionaries could not accept the request to give membership to Swadesh. Ananta once told Naresh that he could keep Swadesh in the party on his own responsibility. But Naresh did not have the courage to take the responsibility. Therefore, Swadesh was not accepted into the party.

Ananta Singh, of course, knew Swadesh well, he used to go to Ganesh's house every day with Debu and Naresh. Swadesh was familiar with the other boys of the team as well. But no one liked Swadesh's sudden arrival.

Swadesh, of course, was not to blame. He often came to this house, when only Ganesh lived there. Today he would not have been able to come in at all if Haripada Mahajan had not gone to drink water for a short while. As soon as Swadesh entered the house, he saw everyone dressed in soldier's uniform and each with a revolver or pistol at his waist; five stun guns and many cartridges were lying open on the bed. In a moment, Swadesh understood the importance of the incident. But when he came in, everyone's faces were filled with annoyance. Ananta and Ganesh looked at Haripada with angry eyes. Haripada stood with his head bowed like a criminal, not knowing what to do.

No one spoke, the room was completely silent. Swadesh could not stand it anymore, realizing this silence. Today he was abandoned by his friends! He seemed to be broken by grief and pride. Yet no one felt any pity for him. Swadesh broke the silence of the room and said - "Did I do anything wrong by coming?" No one answered. He asked again - "Did I do anything wrong?" This time too, he did not get any answer to his question.

The question arises in Ananta's mind if Swadesh is a police spy, then is it necessary to tie him up. If at the last moment the plan fails. Now the question arises in Ananta's mind if he is not a police spy. Although not a party member, Swadesh is a friend of ours.

Now Swadesh noticed everyone's gaze and said - "I made a mistake. Okay, I'll come!" He started walking away, one step at a time. He walked away with deep pain and humiliation. Swadesh may have gone away that day with deep shame.

The time has come for the revolutionaries to come out. Some went out by car and some on foot for the purpose of attacking the Chittagong Armory. As they went, a shadowy figure could be seen in the distance, everyone thought it might be a police officer patrolling. But it was not visible well. The car was moving slowly to get a better look. What is this! This is our swadesh!

Their friend, who was so familiar and so close, seemed to be a stranger to everyone today. The revolutionary friends looked at him, and the homeland looked at its friends. But no one said anything to him. The homeland stood like a stone, its heart a storm raging. Why so much injustice, so much indecent treatment towards it?

On that day Swadesh bore all the neglect of his friends with a closed mouth This time, the car passed by, avoiding him. That day, he kept glancing at his friends' car. No one noticed his thoughts.

After Ananta Singh's group occupied the armory and magazine, they started waiting for Ambika Chakraborty. Ambika Chakraborty would be back with good news in 10 minutes. Everyone looked towards the road to greet them. At that time, a man in white clothes was seen coming from the bend of the waterworks. Who could have come at this time of night, perhaps a policeman from the barracks. Ten revolutionaries raised their guns together and got ready. The party leader gave a loud order - "Hands up! Halt! Who cames there?" The man stood. Then he shouted - "I am Swadesh - I am Swadesh." What? Our Swadesh. To scare Swadesh, they started firing from around him. So that he doesn't get shot. just scaremongering.

But there is no fear of the homeland. Then he said to his friends - "If you still doubt me, whoever you are - dare to shoot me." Instantly, there was a response among the revolutionaries. Everyone was saying that the homeland has arrived! The homeland has arrived! Everyone was overwhelmed with joy. Loud shouts of victory were heard - "Swadesh Roy ki Jai! Bandemataram!" Now his friends welcomed him, and the homeland was welcomed with great joy.

Some handed over rifles, some brought cartridges and some handed over pistols to Swadesha. Ananta Singh went to Swadesha and hugged him tightly. He too hugged him tightly. It was a beautiful sight, despite hundreds of rejections, he dispelled the doubts of the revolutionaries.

But the revolutionaries did not do this injustice to the homeland intentionally. He proved that he was a true patriot. Swadesh had already used breechloader guns. So it didn't take long to train him to use the musket. There two friends trained him to fire a musket. Then they went back to their original purpose.

After 18th April, Swadesh joined the battle of Jalalabad hill on 22nd April. He displayed extraordinary bravery in the historic Battle of Jalalabad Hills, which is rarely compared.

(The rest of it is on pages 54 to 57)

If he had stayed at home that night, without the company of his countrymen, no one would have dared to accuse him of cowardice. Because it was the revolutionaries who had pushed him away.

THE END